Walking
the
Porter Valley

Peter Bayliss, Chris Keeling and Graham Axelby

Acknowledgements

Dr. Kenneth Balkow (flora)
Tony Ball (water power)
Dr. David Crossley (water power)
Peter Kennett (geology)
Dr. Chris Nicholson (ornithology)
Reg Hobson (extra walk)
Sheffield Archive Library

Thanks also to FoPV members, family and friends, who have read various versions,
walked the route and made helpful suggestions.

Further Reading:
Ken Balkow - Wild Plants of the Porter Valley
Muriel Hall - The Mayfield Valley, More of the Mayfield Valley with Old Fulwood
David Hey - A History of Sheffield
Roger Redfern - Fulwood and the Mayfield Valley
Ros Tratt - Bingham Park 1911 to 2011, a Local History
Various leaflets from the Friends of Porter Valley

First published in the United Kingdom by
Arc Publishing and Print 2018

ISBN: 978-1-906722-52-4

Disclaimer: The walking information in this book is given in good faith and is believed to be correct at the time of publication. Neither the authors or the publisher accepts any responsibility for errors or omissions, or for any loss or injury howsoever caused. You alone can judge your own fitness, competence and experience and you should do so before setting out. Walking can be a hazardous activity and only you can judge the level of your own fitness and which walks are suitable for you. It is the responsibility of individuals undertaking outdoor activities to approach the activity with caution and, especially if inexperienced, to do so under supervision. The walks described in this book are not strenuous but individuals should ensure they are suitably fit and correctly dressed before embarking upon them.

Contents

Foreword by
Richard Hawley

In this book you will find a work of dedication, knowledge and love for the Porter Valley. It's well researched and informative for anyone interested in the history, geology, geography and the flora and fauna of the Valley. It's the most concise yet comprehensive book about this Valley I've ever read.

I fell in love with the Porter Valley when I was a boy. We often used to travel from North Sheffield to the cafe at Forge Dam for days out with my family for walks, picnics and hours on the swings and endless goes on the big slide.

I've lived this side of Sheffield for twenty years now but I never tire of it. I enjoy the slow turning of the seasons, the sun, rain (mostly rain), ice and snow. The trees, birds, flowers and the rivers and streams when I'm walking the dogs. I enjoy the cafes too, always nice to have a welcome brew and a butty after a long walk, it helps you take it in, the magic of the place..... Now....where did I put that dog lead and those poo bags?

Photo by Chris Saunders

Introduction

There are several river valleys which flow into Sheffield, Totley Brook, Mayfield Brook, Porter Brook, the rivers Limb, Sheaf, Porter, Rivelin, Loxley and Don. The focus of this book is on two of these, the Porter and Mayfield.

Benefactors

One distinctive feature of the Porter and Mayfield valleys is the impact of benefactors on the Porter Valley. They purchased significant sections of the valley and donated them to the City of Sheffield. Some of the donations were by public subscription such as Endcliffe Park in 1887. Further up the valley Sir John Bingham (Bingham Park) purchased the land in 1911. Other organisations such as the JG Graves Trust donated Carr Bridge to Ringinglow then across to Rycroft Glen, some four miles in extent. Other donations do not name the benefactors, namely the Carr Bridge Path, presented to the City in 1930, the Forge Valley footpath presented to the city in 1933. Most of the donations are marked by large triangular pieces of sandstone grit set on a base of smaller sandstone grit stones.

Trees have also been donated, two in Whiteley Woods dedicated to Alderman Wolstenholm and his wife when they were Lord and Lady Mayoress in 1959. Another tree near Whiteley Wood Road was planted to celebrate the coronation of Edward VII in 1901.

The Porter

The Porter is generally viewed as starting up at Rud Hill, near Brown Edge Quarries and finishing at Hunters Bar. However the river Porter does not end there, it flows into the river Sheaf near Midland Station. The list of mills from Hunter's Bar downstream to the river Sheaf is:- Upper Lescar, Nether Lescar, Snuff Mill, Stalker Wheel, Broomhall Wheel, Broomhall Corn Mill, Norris Wheel, Bennetts Wheel, Sylvester Wheel, Ponds Corn Mill and Lead Mill.

The focus of this book is Hunter's Bar to Brown Edge Quarries, some eight kilometres (five miles) distance with a drop from 425 metres at Rud Hill to 170 metres at Hunter's Bar. The Porter had eight mills in this section of which only Shepherd Mill survives. There were also two corn mills in the Mayfield Valley, one of which survives as a building as part of an animal sanctuary and dog/cat kennels.

The Porter is mainly urban up to Oakbrook Road/Rustlings Road, then less urban and more rural to Carr Bridge, then rural up to Brown Edge Quarries.

The trail is in sections:
Section 1 - Hunter's Bar to Rustlings Road,
Section 2 - Rustlings Road to Hangingwater Road (Whiteley Woods),
Section 3 - Hangingwater Road to Whiteley Wood Road,
Section 4 - Whiteley Wood Bridge to Forge Dam (Brookhouse Hill),
Section 5 - Forge Dam Cafe to Porter Clough / Fulwood Lane and Brown Edge Quarries,
Section 6 - An extra walk around Ringinglow.

The path is rarely a single path, sometimes several options can be taken that eventually meet further up the trail. There are also several deviations from the trail that can be made, these are included. They all lead back to the main trail.

Mayfield Brook

There are no footpaths up the Mayfield Valley. There are lanes which are sometimes near the stream, but the only path is at the Workhouse Cottages which runs by the stream for a very short distance. The source of the May Brook is near Fulwood Lane near the top of Roper Hill.

Information for Visitors

Start: Hunter's Bar Roundabout, junction of Brocco Bank, Ecclesall Road, Junction Road and Sharrow Vale Road.

Finish: Ringinglow, junction of Houndkirk Road, Ringinglow Road and Fulwood Lane.

Description: The River Porter finishes under Midland Station, at the junction where it joins the River Sheaf. It can be walked on a combination of roads and footpaths by the river and through the General Cemetery up to Hunter's Bar. The focus of this walking book has a starting point of Hunter's Bar and continues up to Brown Edge Quarries and Ringinglow. There are many alternatives for starting and finishing points, including starting from Ringinglow and walking downwards towards Hunter's Bar.
There are also many walking (and cycling) alternatives from the Porter Valley, to the Limb Valley, Whirlow, Dore, Totley Moss, Fox House, Grindleford, Stanage Edge, Hathersage, Bamford, Hope, Castleton, Derwent Edge, Strines, Rivelin and so on. The Round Sheffield walk 22 kilometres (14 miles) includes a section from Hunter's Bar to Fulwood Lane. Further afield, at Stanage, is the Sheffield Country Walk (approximately 97 kilometres), which is a full walk round Sheffield.

Maps: For each section, there is a map and also a full length map running from Hunter's Bar to Fulwood Lane. O/S map Landranger 110, OL1 and Explorer 278.

Accessibility: The path from Hunter's Bar to Shepherd Wheel is fairly flat and tarmacked, with easy access for prams and wheelchairs/mobility scooters on some of the paths.
The section from Shepherd Wheel to Forge Dam is steeper and the surfaces, although tarmacked, are not as smooth.
From Forge Dam, the path is mainly hardcore and becomes narrower towards Fulwood Lane. The final section up to Brown Edge Quarries is a footpath over several fields and stiles and is sometimes very muddy.

Public Transport: There are several bus routes which stop at Hunter's Bar, namely 83a (Fulwood and Lodge Moor), 88 (Bents Green), 83 (High Storrs School) and 272 (Castleton). For Forge Dam both the Fulwood (120) and Lodge Moor (83a) stop in Fulwood village. A limited service runs to Ringinglow (4).

Car: At Hunter's Bar, parking is problematic, there are restrictions on parking and there is pressure on nearby roads. Some of the parallel roads to the Porter e.g. Riverdale Road are free of restrictions.
Car parking is more available and less restricted at Forge Dam and at the top (on the left) on Whiteley Lane.
At Fulwood Lane, there is a car park to the south of Porter Clough. Parking is also available at the Norfolk Arms and along Ringinglow Road.

Refreshments: There are many places for refreshments at Hunter's Bar and in the park there is Endcliffe Park Cafe. On Oakbrook Road, just up from the junction with Rustlings Road are two cafes. Further up the valley is Forge Dam Cafe. Much further up and near the top of the valley are the Norfolk Arms at Ringinglow and the Mayfield Valley Alpaca Farm near Ringinglow. Disabled and abled toilets are available at Endcliffe Park Cafe, Forge Dam Cafe and the Norfolk Arms.

Flora of the Porter Valley

Hunter's Bar to Forge Dam

This section of the valley is quite well wooded though there are open areas to the south in Bingham and Endcliffe Parks. The tree canopy contains oak, sycamore, ash and beech with native alder (*Alnus glutinosa*) on the stream bank. The shrub layer has much holly, hawthorn and elder with some mock-orange and snowberry. The last two can be seen in an area below Wire Mill Dam known as "Bowser (Boulsover) Bottom" where there were originally allotment gardens. The streamside herb layer is quite varied with conspicuous flowers such as bluebell, ramsons, wood anemone, wood sorrel, opposite-leaved golden-saxifrage and meadowsweet.

In Endcliffe Park two garden species are established beside the brook, the curious fringe-cups from North America and the blue-flowered trailing bellflower from the Balkans. Woodland natives in Endcliffe Park include sanicle and early dog-violet though both are easy to overlook if not in flower. Ferns are well represented with hard, male and broad buckler-fern abundant beneath the tree canopy and lady fern on the stream bank. The rarer soft shield-fern occurs occasionally, for example on the bank opposite the Shepherd Wheel.

The vegetation beside the restored Shepherd Wheel millpond is still developing but already contains large specimens of pendulous sedge with its drooping female flowers.

Ramsons

Forge Dam to Brown Edge Quarries

The surroundings of Forge Dam are still well wooded though the marshy area to the west (known as the Sorby Plantation) is unsafe to enter and warning signs are posted. A noteworthy new arrival at Forge Dam is the American species large-leaved avens which is not only spreading but also hybridising with our native wood avens.

Beyond Carr Bridge the valley is more open though the stream is still bordered by alder and sycamore trees. The non-native grey alder (*Alnus incana*) has also been planted in Porter Clough. A colony of great horsetail to the west of Carr Bridge continues to expand but smaller species such as pink purslane still find a foothold amongst it.

East of Carr Bridge the yellow flowers of tansy and tall melilot can be seen along the bridleway, and along Clough Lane the aniseed-scented umbellifer sweet cicely flowers in May. This part of the valley is surrounded by permanent pasture but some fields through which public footpaths pass have not undergone agricultural improvement. These are good places to view colourful meadow plants such as marsh ragwort, devilsbit scabious, bulbous buttercup, lesser spearwort and heath milkwort.

Two unusual grasses occur in this part of the valley, wood barley and wood fescue. The latter inhabits a slope opposite Forge Dam whilst the former is mainly seen near the waterfall in Porter Clough.

Some escaped or discarded garden plants occur here or on road verges in the upper Mayfield Valley. Typical examples are purple cranesbill on Greenhouse Lane, and honesty, perennial cornflower and green alkanet on Clough Lane. West of Fulwood Lane the brook flows down Clough Hollow and is bordered by moorland shrubs such as heather, bilberry and western gorse. Where the footpath meets the stream below Brown Edge Farm are a few garden plants such as Hidcote Comfrey and three-cornered garlic, both probably introduced by accident during pipe-laying work.

Large - leaved Avens

Soft Shield-fern

Fringe-cups

Pendulous Sedge

Sweet Cicely

The Birds of the Porter Valley

The valley provides a number of different environments which cater for the needs of a wide variety of birds. But it is the River Porter itself which is at the centre and indeed was the creator of the valley which should be the first habitat to be considered. The river feeds into a number of dams and mill ponds which are home to ducks and other water birds.

By far the most common duck is the Mallard and having a wide breeding season, some seem to be able to produce two or even three broods in a single season. This gives the opportunity of seeing both young ducklings growing and also the adult ducks in eclipse plumage.

Other ducks regularly seen are Teal, Goosander, Dabchick and the exotic Mandarin. Perhaps originally escapees from collections this lovely duck in now known to breed in the valley. Moorhen and Coot can be seen in most of the dams throughout the valley.

Other water birds include the brightest of all, the Kingfisher. Although often only seen as a flash of brilliant colour over a dam it can also be seen even as high as Carr Bridge. The state of the river and the fish it provides must influence the population and range of the bird.

Herons are frequently seen throughout the valley both in river and the dams. They are also seen over nearby houses in the vicinity of Fulwood and Ranmoor, perhaps attracted by the number of garden ponds offering a ready source of food. Other birds feed along the river such as the Grey Wagtail and the Dipper. Both are present throughout the year and can be seen hopping from stone to stone and in the case of the Dipper, living up to its name, by diving under the water and walking against the currents in search of the small invertebrates which abound in the river. Both have characteristic calls as they work the river and you may be lucky to hear the Dipper in song very early in the year as it calls for mates and establishes its territory.

There are a good population of common birds such as Robins, Wrens, Blackbirds, Thrushes, both Song and Mistle and the full range of tits, Blue, Great, Coal and Long-Tailed. There is always a possibility of seeing a Willow Tit, though these are less common and rarely seen in the valley. Other families regularly seen are the finches, Chaffinch, Bullfinch, Greenfinch, Goldfinch and the slightly smaller Siskin, are all beautiful birds with distinctive plumage and calls. We are also fortunate to have both the Green Woodpecker and the Great Spotted Woodpecker resident in the valley. The Lesser Spotted Woodpecker once seen in the valley seems to have left us for the moment.

A Kingfisher at Ibbotson Wheel - Photo by Ian Slingsby

One group of birds which always causes excitement, both for bird watchers and for the birds themselves, are the birds of prey. The Kestrel, which hovers overhead in search of small mammals, is the most easily recognised and is the most common. However both Sparrow Hawk and increasingly Buzzard are seen and heard in the valley. Buzzards are often seen in pairs and later in the season perhaps in greater numbers. They can be frequently heard mewing to each other as they glide on the breeze high above our heads. The red kite has been increasing in numbers throughout the country and on one memorable occasion was seen gliding over the upper part of the valley close to Porter Clough. Tawny Owls are very common in the valley, identified by their readily copied call, and the rarer Little Owl has been known to breed in the valley.

All of the above birds can be seen throughout the year , but the valley also provides the keen ornithologist with a whole new range of both summer and winter visitors. Dealing first with summer visitors, perhaps the warblers provides the first change in the seasons. The Chiff-Chaff is invariably the first to appear readily identified by its onomatopoeic call which gives its name. This is usually followed by the Willow Warbler an almost identical appearance to the Chiff-Chaff but with a delightful gently descending call.

Other warblers follow such as the Blackcap, Whitethroat, Garden Warbler, Grasshopper Warbler, Sedge Warbler and if we are lucky the Wood Warbler. All of these birds have distinctive calls which have to be learnt and rememorized each year. Frequently it is the only way of identifying the species as the growing leaves make positive spotting more and more difficult. In recent years there have been several sightings of the Blackcap over the winter months. Perhaps global warming is encouraging some to remain with us throughout the year.

The most eagerly awaited summer visitor is the Swallow closely followed by the House Martin and if we are lucky , accompanied by the odd Sand Martin, but these do not seem to want to stay within the valley. The last aerial feeder to appear, and the first to leave is the Swift, readily identified by its curved wing shape and screaming call.

Spotted Flycatchers are also regular visitors, but tend to be seen higher up the valley near the river source. A single record has also been made of a Pied Flycatcher

A Kingfisher just below Carr Bridge

again in this area. This could be one which lost its way as they are regular visitors to Padley Gorge over he moors in Derbyshire. The area of the valley close to the moors attracts a different group of birds, most notably the Curlew with its distinctive warbling call which carries over great distances. Other species in this area include the Golden Plover, Woodcock, Redstart and Snipe.

Autumn prompts the departure of the summer visitors, it also heralds the arrival of the winter visitors to the valley. Both Redwing and the slightly larger Fieldfare are in the thrush family and they both leave the cooler climes of Scandinavia for our slightly warmer winter months. They are seen in the valley and tend to feed in the fields and on the numerous berried bushes which are distributed throughout the valley.

It would also appear that valley is used as a navigational aid to these and other species. On one occasion over a period of perhaps half an hour a flock of Redwing and Fieldfare, which possibly numbered up to a thousand birds, were using the valley and its river as a compass bearing to the west. A truly amazing sight. Other migrant flocks of finches and Brambling have also been noted.

One family not yet mentioned are the corvids or Crows. The three common species are the Carrion Crow, the Rook and the Jackdaw. The valley has two rookeries one ar Wire Mill and the other at Forge Dam. Graham Sedgewick, a local enthusiastic and very committed bird watcher has been surveying the numbers of rooks in these areas over the last 30 years and his figures show a considerable reduction at both sites over this period. In the mid 1980s he counted 150 Rook nests at Forge Dam and 100 at Wire Mill. Current figures of 49 at Forge Dam and just 13 at Wire Mill are somewhat disturbing. Large numbers of these birds can be seen in the daytime out on the fields high in the valley and their return to roost in the evening is always a spectacular sight. Without accurate data from all the other local sites it is not possible to determine the cause of these reductions.

Is this due to a general reduction in birdlife in the valley or have the rooks just decided to move to other sites?

The valley provides an environment of interest to birdwatchers throughout the year. An observant walker through the valley can almost be guaranteed a sighting of between 25 to 30 species at any time of the year.

A Dipper

A Little Grebe (Dab Chick)

A Mandarin Duck

A Heron in Porter Brook

Dams of the Porter Valley

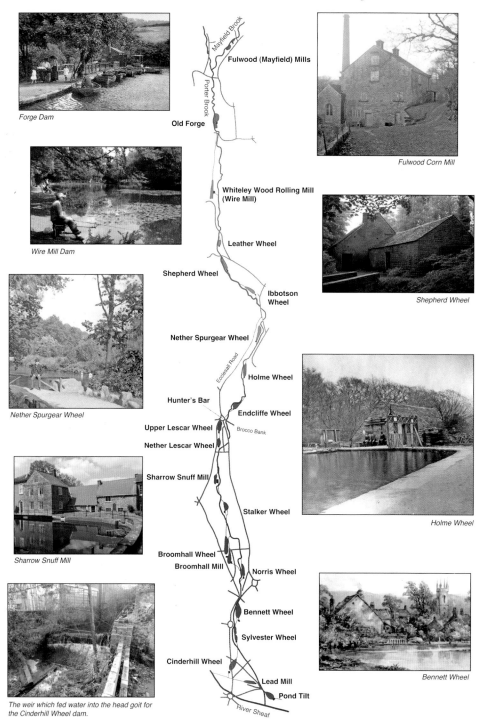

Forge Dam

Fulwood (Mayfield) Mills

Old Forge

Fulwood Corn Mill

Wire Mill Dam

Whiteley Wood Rolling Mill (Wire Mill)

Leather Wheel

Shepherd Wheel

Ibbotson Wheel

Shepherd Wheel

Nether Spurgear Wheel

Nether Spurgear Wheel

Holme Wheel

Hunter's Bar

Endcliffe Wheel

Upper Lescar Wheel

Nether Lescar Wheel

Sharrow Snuff Mill

Stalker Wheel

Holme Wheel

Sharrow Snuff Mill

Broomhall Wheel

Broomhall Mill

Norris Wheel

Bennett Wheel

Sylvester Wheel

Cinderhill Wheel

Lead Mill

Pond Tilt

Bennett Wheel

The weir which fed water into the head goit for the Cinderhill Wheel dam.

The influence of the Geology upon the scenery

In general terms, the relief of an area is largely dictated by the resistance to erosion of the rocks which lie underneath it. More resistant rocks usually form the higher ground, and less resistant ones occupy the valleys and lower ground.
In our area, the more resistant rocks are the sandstones, and the weaker ones are the shales, siltstones and coal seams.

The geological structure of the rocks also exerts an influence on the landscape, and much depends upon the direction in which the rocks were tilted by earth movements, maybe millions of years after they were deposited.
In our area, the rocks are generally tilted to the east or northeast, forming the eastern part of a major "dome" structure affecting much of the South Pennines. However, in Sheffield itself, there is another influence, which reaches as far as Nether Edge. This is the extensive fold known as the Don Monocline, which roughly follows the course of the lower Don river. (A monocline is a fold where one limb is much steeper than the other, to the point where it is vertical. A small example of a monocline can be seen in the river banks 100 metres or so south of Forge Dam).

The effect of the Don Monocline is to produce an S- shaped outcrop for the Green-moor Rock and for the younger sandstones above it. The Greenmoor Rock snakes its way from Homebase on Chesterfield Road to form Brincliffe Edge. It then crosses the Porter and continues on its way northwards to Huddersfield.

Sometimes, rocks became fractured and displaced by faults, as well as folded, and there are several places in the valley where such faults occur. Their presence is often only detected by careful mapping of the outcrops, both above ground and in mines and quarries, but there are places where their influence on the landscape is more apparent.

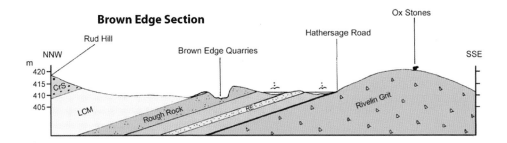

The Porter Valley route

Hunter's Bar

Endcliffe Wheel

Mi Amigo Memorial

Holme Wheel

Endcliffe Park

Endcliffe Park Cafe

Situated by the river and the open play area, this pavilion style cafe offers something for all the family.

Seasonal, Home-Made Specials. All Fair Trade Coffee

Open from 9am - 5pm

Snacks, sandwiches, milkshakes, smoothies, ice creams, hot and cold drinks can all be bought either to take away or eat in.

Porter Brook

Rustlings Rd

Rustlings-Road Allotments

Nether Spurgear Wheel

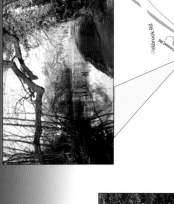

Oakbrook Rd

Westmead Rd

Ibbotson Wheel

Porter Brook

Shepherd Wheel

Hangingwater Rd

Whiteley Wood Rd

Leather Wheel

Hangingwater Rd

Whiteley Wood Rd

Thomas Boulsover Memorial

Porter Brook

Wire Mill

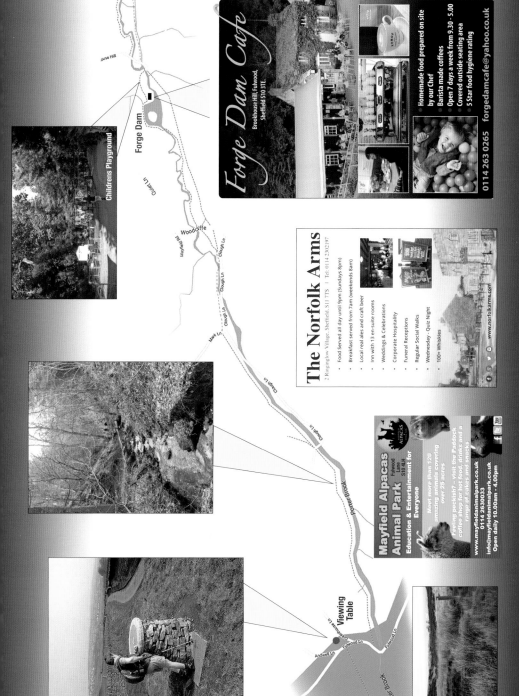

Childrens Playground

Forge Dam

Louse Hill

Quiet Ln

Woodcliffe

Mayfield Rd

Clough Ln

Clough Ln

Clough Ln

Clough Ln

Clough Ln

Porter Brook

Viewing Table

Andrew Ln

Fulwood Ln

Fulwood Ln

Fulwood Ln

Rud Hill

Porter Brook

The Porter Valley

The Porter Valley is a three-mile long finger of green open space linking the inner suburbs of Sheffield to the countryside. A series of public footpaths, bridleways, and cycle-ways follow the river from Hunter's Bar to Fulwood Head. From these you experience two designed city parks, woodlands, an Urban Nature Park at Common Lane, picturesque landscape of farms, hills, smaller woods and fields where, in summer, cows stand knee deep in buttercups. The footpath network enables circular walks to be followed away from the valley bottom.

A landscaped shaped by geology and mankind, the sequence being; metal trades and farming, waterpower to the 18th century beginning of the industrial revolution, population growth, emergence of the city out of the hamlets and the 1880s social conscience / parkification.

A feature of the valley is the remains of water-powered industry in the form of six mill ponds (dams) and goits that once provided water to drive grindstones, forge-hammers and wiremills. Shepherd Wheel is a unique example on the valley of a cutlers work shop. Medieval and earlier field patterns, deep hollow-ways, rig and furrow, and 'socket and groove' gate posts together with other wall furniture signal man's shaping of the landscape.

Throughout the valley a wealth of natural history is present at all times of the year. Much of it is concentrated on the mill ponds with the ducks, herons, water lilies and fish, while the woodland is alive with song birds and in spring the paths are edged with an attractive flora. Away from the valley bottom there are species-rich grasslands, attractive hedgerows, flowery road verges, veteran trees and sheltered lanes favoured by butterflies.

What both regular users and occasional visitors appreciate about the valley is its tranquillity, naturalness, ease of access, and the variety of experience it has to offer.

The Friends of the Porter Valley environmental group was set up in July 1994 and registered as a charity in 1995.

A recent vision statement reads "to conserve, protect, and restore the ecology, landscape and cultural heritage of the Porter and Mayfield Valleys for the enjoyment of all and the benefit of future generations." Several projects have been undertaken and completed, namely Endcliffe Park play area, Adult Gym, Parkour and Shepherd Wheel restorations.

The projects for 2018 are the restoration of Bingham Park, Forge Dam, the play area at Forge Dam and improvements to the entrance at Hunter's Bar.

Support for the above projects has come from a number of sources:- from membership fees, donations, legacies, community events such as the Duck Race, the Autumn and Christmas Fairs, the Co-op, Heritage Lottery Fund, Sheffield City Council, Sheffield Industrial Museums Trust, Section 106 funding, to name some. Maintenance work is carried out twice monthly, by conservation volunteers, in Endcliffe Park, Whiteley Woods, Shepherd Wheel, Forge Dam, Common Lane Open Space, Jubilee Wood and above Fulwood Lane near Brown Edge Quarries. Pupils from Nether Green Junior School were involved in a conservation project through the planting a number of young native trees, by the river, above Fulwood Lane.

Planning issues that may impact on the Porter and Mayfield Valleys, are also reviewed.

Open meetings are held every three months with speakers covering a range of local topics. There are also organised walks featuring local history, the dawn chorus, bats, flowers, medicinal plants, geology, etc.

The web-site is: www.fopv.org.uk

Friends of the Porter Valley booklets

The Porter Valley – Wildlife and History, Issue 2 2006.

Delving into the past.
Mining and Quarrying in the Porter Valley. Peter Kennett.

The Geology of the Porter Valley –
what lies beneath our feet? Peter Kennett.

Reading the Landscape in the Porter Valley.

Industrial and Social History of the Porter Valley

Registered Charity No. 1069865

1/ Hunter's Bar to Rustlings Road

Distance: **1.1km. (0.7 miles)**
Difficulty: **Easy-going, tarmac path, suitable for wheelchairs, three short slopes.**
Facilities: **Cafe, toilets and children's playground (Please note, the next public toilets on the walk are approximately three kilometres (two miles) away at Forge Dam).**
Buses: **Routes 4, 81, 82, 83, 83a, 88 and 272 to Hunter's Bar.**
Parking: **Short-term on-street parking is available on Ecclesall Road and Sharrowvale Road. A limited amount of parking is available in the park, entry from Rustlings Road, next to the junction with Ecclesall Road.**

The walk begins at Hunter's Bar. The name is taken from the toll-bar that once stood where the traffic roundabout now stands. It was the last toll-bar in Sheffield to close, at midnight on the 30th October 1884. As midnight approached, a crowd gathered, and on the stroke of midnight, they tore down the toll-gate and threw it

into nearby fields. The following year the first part of the area which became Endcliffe Park was acquired by the Council, and the substantial gateposts from the toll-bar were used at the entrance. In the 1950s the junction was substantially remodelled, along with the park entrance and adjacent part of the park, and the gateposts were returned to their original position, on the roundabout, where they still stand.

Inside the park, on the left, stands the former tearoom and keeper's lodge, now the base for the park rangers. Its provision in 1893 was not without opposition in Council, the cost having risen to exceed the £1,000 agreed. There was also much discussion as to whether refreshment facilities should be available to the public.

Ahead the path divides, and in the angle stands a statue of Queen Victoria, originally erected outside the Town Hall in May 1905, and moved to its present location in February 1930.

Take the path to the right, over the small footbridge and round to the left. This part of the Porter Brook was canalised in the alterations in the 1950s.

Where the footbridge now crosses the brook was formerly an ornate sheltered drinking fountain.
Inside was an elaborate bronze fountain with three goblets on chains, and a drinking trough for dogs. It was presented in August 1889 by Mrs W.G. Blake in memory of her late father, Thomas Jessop.

With the Porter Brook on the left, to the right is a raised, flat grassed area. This is the site of a dam serving the Endcliffe Wheel, the first of three in this section of the walk.

Endcliffe Wheel

A grinding workshop, the wheel dates from 1706, when it was known as Elcliffe Wheel.
It operated until the 1880s. Shortly afterwards the surrounding land, along with the wheel and dam, were acquired by the Council and became a public park. The dam became a bathing pool (for men and boys only), and was the centre of much controversy due to complaints of 'foul language and lewd behaviour' on the part of bathers and onlookers. It remained a bathing pool until 1938. During World War 2 it served as an emergency water supply for the fire service, after which it was filled in and landscaped, along with the now disappeared remains of the Wheel.

The pool closed in 1938 and was finally drained and landscaped in the 1950s.

The inscription reads:

The adjoining land, to the extent of nine acres, was purchased by subscription and presented to the corporation of Sheffield for the purpose of a Public Recreation Ground in commemoration of the Jubilee of
Her Majesty Queen Victoria
1887

Cross a small bridge and bear right. The route continues past the playground, cafe and toilets. On the left is an open space where linear undulations can be seen. These are the vestiges of ridge and furrow cultivation, remnants of Rustlings Farm which stood roughly at what is now the junction of Rustlings Road and Ecclesall Road. Near the cafe, the brook is crossed by a row of large stepping stones. These were placed as part of the 'parkification' by Goldring, a renowned urban landscape architect in the 1880s and have been much loved and remembered by generations of children as a favourite place to play and paddle in the brook. In their early days they were also much beloved by postcard companies, photographed from all angles, with and without children, in sunlight, snow and in one postcard,' by moonlight' with children playing on the stones! (see page 59)

On the hillside to the right, beyond the cafe and across the brook, is a memorial to the crew of an American B17 aircraft, Mi Amigo.

Did you know (Mi Amigo)

There is a war memorial in Endcliffe Park? On the hillside across the brook behind the cafe is a memorial to an event that happened during the World War 2.

On the afternoon of the 22nd February 1944, a badly damaged B17 bomber, called Mi Amigo, of the 305th Bomb Group based at Chelverston, emerged from the

overcast skies and crashed into the hillside. All ten members of the crew were killed. There are many stories and accounts of the crash, which is commemorated by the memorial on the site, and on the anniversary wreaths are laid by the people of Sheffield and members of the United States Air Force, followed by a service in the nearby St Augustine's Church on Brocco Bank. A detailed account can be found here https://h2g2.com/edited_entry/A7563783 , and there is a book about the events by a local author, David Harvey, entitled "Mi Amigo, the story of Sheffield's Flying Fortress."

Almost opposite the cafe, near where the outside seating is now, there previously stood a bandstand, once a feature of many of Sheffield's parks, though few still exist. On the 3rd August 1899, the Sheffield Independent reported that the benefit concerts held in the parks had raised money for the support of seven Sheffield bands, Endcliffe raising the most with £42.

Continuing past the cafe and toilets the route bears right up a short slope passing a small cascade on the right, part of the landscaping by Goldring and the outflow from the next dam which served the Holme or Second Endcliffe Wheel.

A George Cunningham painting depicting the bandstand and cafe in Endcliffe Park.

*The Friends of Porter Valley annual duck race which is held every Easter.
The ducks race down the Porter, with the help of children with sticks, to the finishing
line just below Endcliffe Park Cafe.*

On the far side of the dam is an open area. This is the site of the only known fireclay workings in the Porter Valley. Records from 1825 show a small area of workings, only 0.1 acres in extent, and it isn't clear whether this was worked by underground mining or opencast. Whichever method was used, there are no visible traces left. The 1825 records give a value of £200 for the site.

Past the head of the dam and the associated weir there is another open space on the left with traces of ridge and furrow while on the hillside on the other side of the brook is part of Smith Wood, a remnant of ancient woodland.

The route continues beside the Porter on your right until it passes another cascade (on the left) and rises up a short slope to the next dam.

This served the Nether Spurgear Wheel, and by the path near the cascade is a marker showing the location of the wheel, of which no traces remain.

Holme Wheel

Nether Spurgear Wheel

2/ Rustlings Road to Hangingwater Bridge
(Whiteley Woods)

Distance: **0.9km. (0.6 miles)**
Difficulty: **Easy-going, tarmac path, suitable for wheelchairs. One short incline at Hangingwater Bridge. Please be aware that this section of the path is shared with a marked cycle track, and parts of the path, though tarmac, can be muddy at times due to down-wash from the hillside.**
Facilities: **None, but cafes nearby on Oakbrook Road at Nether Green.**
Buses: **83a**
Parking: **On-street on Oakbrook Road and Riverdale Road.**

The section begins at the junction of Rustlings Road and Oakbrook Road. If you are lucky you may see a few trout that congregate below the bridge. The route passes through Whiteley Woods, quickly changing from parkland to woodland. Within it are the sites of two grinding wheels, Ibbotson Wheel and Shepherd Wheel. The latter was restored to working order in 2012 and is open to the public every weekend and Bank Holiday Mondays.
Immediately after passing the former park keeper's lodge on the left, a footpath climbs the hill, passing an open space which, in spring, is covered by a host of daffodils. Once beyond the trees this area opens out into Bingham Park.

> **Did you know** Bingham Park covers 11 acres of the hillside above this part of Whiteley Woods. It was given to the city by Sir John Bingham in 1911. It was originally part of the grounds of the 18th century Greystones Hall. Sir John was a partner in the Sheffield firm of Walker and Hall. The story goes that he offered his wife Maria the choice of a set of jewels, or to give the land which became the park to the city. Lady Bingham decided that the children of Sheffield should have a park. Sir John was a believer in the beneficial effects of the open air, being involved in the opening of the Botanical Gardens to the general public, and the building of the Peace Gardens next to the Town Hall.
> The story surrounding the circumstances of the gift of the park and its history is told in a booklet "Bingham Park 1911-2011, a History".

Continuing along the path in the valley bottom, the mown grass area gives into woodland, i.e. Whiteley Woods.

> **Did you know**
> The first house on Oakbrook Road, visible through the trees on the right, was the setting for a murder in the book Silent Playgrounds by local author Danuta Reah. The victim's body was subsequently found in the wheelpit at Shepherd Wheel, a 'fact' that occasionally brings a shudder to visitors at the Wheel who have read the book!

The path soon joins the brook which can be crossed by a small bridge which in turn leads to a path and steps by which you can climb the embankment which forms the dam wall. (Wheelchair access is via the far end of the dam). This dam served the Ibbotson Wheel. Built in 1750, only the shuttle and overflow still exist. In 1850 it had the dubious distinction of being the only wheel in this area to suffer rattening, in which £40 of tools were destroyed.

Did you know

The shelter in Whiteley Woods was built about the sixties. As youths we used to listen to Radio Luxembourg in the new shelter on transistor radios.

It was built as a public shelter and a rest room for the park keepers who also had lockers in there.

The lock up store was sometimes used for mowers and other machines. They used to have a snowplough on two wheels to clear the paths.

At that time there were nine park keepers based there (Porter Glen) in the long summer daylight hours, two men would work on the Bingham park golf course, two on the top tennis courts, two on the bowling greens and two on the bottom tennis courts alongside Oakbrook Road. The head park keeper lived in the lodge that has now been sold off.

There were also two men permanently at Forge Dam as they had to patrol as far as Fulwood Lane.

In Endcliffe Park the number could have been even higher.

In the shorter days when the games were not in use the men would work on major tasks for the winter, planting trees, laying paths, building steps and digging out Forge.

(Roger Kay, pers.comm.)

Ibbotson Wheel.
The first lease for this wheel is in 1754. At a later date the dam was extended. In 1827 the wheel suffered rattening, and five grindstones were broken. By 1900 the wheel was owned by Sheffield Corporation, and in 1902 the Ibbotson family were given notice to quit. The building was still in fair condition in 1930, when it was suggested it, together with the Shepherd Wheel, might become an industrial museum. The wheel was eventually demolished in 1950.

The wheel was in good order in 1930, when it was suggested that, along with Shepherd Wheel, it could become an industrial museum, though nothing came of the idea. It was demolished in 1950, and the site is now occupied by a small copse of trees hiding a national grid gas pressure monitor.

The dam was altered slightly in the 1970s by the addition of a small island for waterfowl. Like most others in the valley, the dam is now heavily silted.

(continued)
and in the Sheffield Independent of 27th June 1896, an advertisement appeared for *"PORTER GLEN, TOP OF ENDCLIFFE PARK - Visitors will find Good Accommodation for Hot Water; Teas Provided, Schools and parties Catered for; Boating, Swings; a large Play Ground - W.C IBBOTSON."*
A again, in the same newspaper for 21st July 1900,
"PORTER GLEN, Beautifully situated in Endcliffe Woods. School Treats and Parties catered for; swings and boating. W.C Ibbotson."
However, Walter may still have been continuing his original trade, as a year later in the census of 1901, he was still residing at 145 Oakbrook Road, but was now described as 'File grinder and shopkeeper confectioner.'
According to the records, Walter died in 1907, but the business seems to have continued, as it was still listed in the trade directory for 1911. According to local people there was still a motor boat giving rides on the dam certainly up to the 1930s.

Rejoin the main path either by retracing your steps, or by the bridge at the top end of the dam, and continue alongside the brook. After a short distance it brings you to Shepherd Wheel.

Shepherd Wheel

This scheduled ancient monument was first recorded in a will of 1584 and was restored to working order in 2012, and is exactly as it was when it ceased production in the 1930s, though the interior and the machinery are as they would have been for very many years before that. The Wheel is open to the public every weekend and Bank Holiday Mondays. Opening times and more information can be found at http://www.fopv.org.uk/shepherd%20wheel.htm and admission is free. It is owned by the City Council, and operated by the Sheffield Industrial Museums Trust, with the help of volunteers from the Friends of the Porter Valley. There are no facilities, but all parts are accessible by wheelchair.

This section ends at Hangingwater Bridge, which is at the far end of the dam. It can be reached either via the main path, which has a short incline, or by walking along the dam, ending in a flight of steps. The latter route gives a view of the double weir, part of the water management system.

Shepherd Wheel Dam

The Geology

Shepherd Wheel (SK317853); Rough Rock; Pot Clay Shales

Shepherd Wheel is the most historic of all the former cutlery works in the Porter Valley. The mill dam is sited immediately downstream of the road bridge over the River Porter, where Hangingwater Road/Highcliffe Road cross the river.

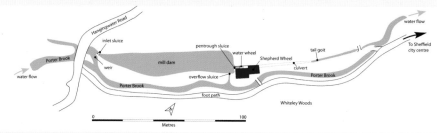

A good sequence of different beds can be seen in the river banks, by walking downstream on the tarmac footpath on the south side of the river, between Highcliffe Road and the end of the iron railings. To get the best view you need to get in the river itself, but a reasonable understanding can be obtained from the safety of the path! Because of the north-easterly dip of the rocks, the oldest units occur nearest to the road bridge and the youngest further downstream.

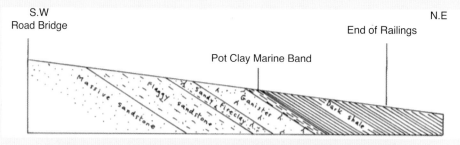

Sketch geological section of the beds in the river banks at Shepherd Wheel. Length of section about 100metres. Dip exaggerated.

About 20 metres upstream of the end of the railings, a holly tree stands on the opposite (north bank). This is growing out of a thick sandstone unit, and the roots can be seen opening up the joints. Close examination shows that the sandstone is an excellent ganister, which when fresh is a pale grey colour with black plant rootlets scattered throughout. It is extremely hard and must have taken a lot of grinding down when it was used to make refractory bricks for the steel industry.

The foundations of the Hangingwater Road bridge stand on relatively massive, cross-bedded sandstones, belonging to the Rough Rock.

A few metres downstream, the river flows over what appears to be a sloping concrete slab, but this is, in fact, a bedding plane in the sandstone. This can be confirmed by studying the section in the stream bank a little further downstream, which shows a series of thin harder sandstones alternating with softer siltstones.

Ganister, beneath holly roots near Shepherd Wheel.
(hammer 30cm long)

A ganister represents a fossil soil and is usually found below a coal seam, the tree growth having removed all the elements apart from the silica. This means that we ought to find a coal seam sitting on top of the ganister, but we are in for a surprise! On the north bank, the ganister is partly covered by the man-made embankment of the Shepherd Wheel Dam, so nothing more is visible. However, if you are prepared to paddle, you can trace the ganister laterally across to the south bank and continue to follow the succession upwards (i.e. downstream). No coal appears! Instead, there is a sequence of extremely crumbly, dirty shales.

A very careful search may reveal the very poorly fossilised remains of bivalves and goniatites, occupying only a few centimetres of shales. These were marine creatures and they are proof that the sea must have flooded into this region soon after the ganister had been deposited.

We shall never know if a coal seam had formed first and then been washed away, although elsewhere in the Yorkshire coalfield a coal seam does occur at this level in the succession.

Leather Wheel

3/ Hangingwater Bridge to Whiteley Wood Road

Distance: **1.1km (0.7 miles)**
Difficulty: **Easy going tarmac path with two short inclines at the beginning and end.**
Facilities: **None.**
Buses: **None.**
Parking: **On-street on Whiteley Wood Road, near the junction with Hangingwater Road. (Cross Hangingwater Road and rejoin the route at the bridge.)**

This is the shortest section of the route. Before leaving the bridge look over the wall facing upstream. This was the site of the next Wheel, variously known as Leather Wheel.

Tree roots of Carboniferous age (SK315853); Rough Rock

About 80 metres southwest up from the road bridge which carries Highcliffe Road/ Hangingwater Road over the Porter, there is a silted up mill dam, known formerly as Leather Wheel. Rocks are exposed in the low cliff to the north of the old dam. The cliff was probably steepened by quarrying for stone for the dams and it is best approached from the point where the mill stream passes under the tarmac path.

The geological unit at this point still consists of the ubiquitous Rough Rock, its outcrop having been continued this far down the valley by faulting.

Some of the sandstone blocks which make up the cliff have clearly slipped somewhat, but a few remain more or less in their true position. Careful examination of these will reveal a number of stippled, roughly cylindrical shapes cutting across the bedding of the sandstone. These are the remains of tree stumps and roots, of Carboniferous age. The original wood has long since decayed, but the imprint of the bark has been preserved in the sandstone.

Leather Wheel

Built in 1754, it ceased operation around 1900, and was finally demolished in 1907. Although he didn't build it, a few years after it opened it was incorporated into the works of Thomas Boulsover, whose name will crop up again later. The site has been landscaped, but it is possible to see where the wheelpit stood, and the water management that feeds Shepherd Wheel. The name Leather  *Wheel is suggested to have referred to its use at one time for grinding alder bark for use in the tanning industry.*

At the right-hand end of the bridge there is a stile in the wall, leading to a narrow Holloway. This is the former Porter Lane that led from Fulwood to the bridge. Only this lower section remains, the rest having disappeared under Woofindin Road, which follows roughly the same line.

Rejoin the path which rises over a bridge to run along an embankment above the river. This is the wall of the dam which served Leather Wheel: the dam itself was filled in in 1954 except for a channel which runs beside the path. Originally it filled the space between the path and the bank running up to Whiteley Wood Road. The arched outflow passes under the path, and the entry shuttle can still be seen at the top of the goit, next to the weir. Across the river is an area of woodland, Bluebell Wood, through which an ochre brook runs to join the Porter below the weir.

The bridge by which Whiteley Wood Road crosses the Porter is unusual. Examination from below (not recommended!) shows the original sandstone arch sandwiched between two brick extensions, the result of widening in the 19th Century. Photos of the bridge from the early 20th century show the sides of the bridge formed of a lattice of branches, now replaced with stone. It is the ends of the bridge which are distinctive and give it its local name of the "armchair bridge". At each end of the bridge, on both sides, are buttresses, into which are set stone seats, hence the name.

1906

Boulsover Chapel Diversion

From the armchair bridge, turn left as if to walk back down the valley on the other side of the river. About 30 metres on your right take the path which follows the small brook upwards. This is Bluebell Wood. Eventually the path meets another coming from the left. Turn right through a stile and follow the fence on your left. You will probably hear the brook in the trees beyond the fence. The brook rises in the bank above Trap Lane, behind Meadow Farm, and feeds a small trough in the dip of the lane. Here it is clear, but by the time it reaches the Porter near the armchair bridge it is orange from the iron deposits in the soil. (It is unusual in the area by having no name.) Keeping the fence on your left, walk up the large field until you reach some metal railings. This field was formerly the playing field belonging to King Edward VII school. Turn right and follow the railings until you reach the road (Whiteley Wood Road). Turn left up the hill and just before you reach Meadow Lane Farm there is a small stone building. Now very dilapidated and in need of attention, this is the Boulsover Chapel. It was built in 1789 by the daughters of Thomas Boulsover, who, with his family, lived nearby at Whiteley Wood Hall. There is a plaque marking the chapel, which is a listed building. Originally intended as a place of worship for the workers at Boulsover's works and estate in the valley, it eventually fell into disuse, and has since served as a cow house and a store. Inside there is very little evidence of its original purpose.

Boulsover Chapel (Local Studies ref s06165)

Cross the road, turn left, and continue on the path by the road. At the sharp bend to the left, turn right down Ivy Cottage Lane. The lane winds down into the valley to rejoin the walk at Forge Dam.

By a bend half way down the lane a stream passes under the road, and the lane is joined by a footpath from Priest Hill via a stile. In the field on the left is a small group of trees. These are growing from the ruined remains of a small farmhouse, Lower Priest Hill Farm. Further down the lane, again on the left, a building is visible through the trees. This is the former Cottage Lane School, now a private residence.

Whiteley Wood School around 1900

On the last bend before the bottom of the lane, there is evidence of another habitation. Under the roots of a large tree growing on the bank, is a round wooden door, with the words "Chestnut, Plane & Sycamore, Who or What Lies Beyond the Door?" Some believe it's a hobbit house, others that it's the house of the Gruffalo. What do you think? Spoiler alert: a few years ago the bank was in danger of collapse bringing down the tree.

It was stabilised with concrete, which was unsightly, so local craftsman and ex-council ranger Henk Littlewood was commissioned to carry out the work and create the doorway to an imaginary world!!

At the bottom of the lane you rejoin the original route.

Did you know (Whiteley Wood Hall)

The original hall was built by Thomas Dale between 1663-5, he had two daughters one of who married Alexander Ashton from Stoney Middleton. Alexander remodelled the hall but the family became extinct and the Hall was passed onto Strelley Pegge of Beauchief. The hall was then sold to Thomas Boulsover, who was the inventor of Sheffield Silver Plate. Thomas Boulsover already owned large areas of land around Whiteley Woods including Wire Mill & Forge Dam. Boulsover died at the hall in 1788, and was survived by two daughters, one being Mrs Hutton who took on the ownership of the house with her husband who died in 1818. The house remained in the family until 1864 when it was bought by Mr Plimsoll. He was responsible for the law that required a line around a ship that must not go below water level when the ship is loaded. In 1868 the South Yorkshire Miners Association held a rally for 10,000 people at the hall and gardens. In 1893 the hall became the home to Arnold Muir Wilson & family who were solicitors from Sheffield. In 1896 Sheffield Council purchased the hall. In 1903 the hall was purchased for the use as an outdoor activity centre. In 1920 Vickers Ltd bought the hall with William Clarke and his family taking up residence, Vickers using the hall for entertaining. In 1926 Vickers sold the hall to Sheaf Investment Co and from that date the hall went into a steady decline until 1959 when it was demolished.

All that remains today are the stables that the Girl Guides and other organisations use, Whiteley Wood Manor and three cottages.

The old outbuildings and stable block, now used as an outdoor activity centre.

A family making their way over the stepping stones just after Whiteley Wood Bridge.

4/ Whiteley Wood Bridge to Forge Dam

Distance: **1.1km (0.7 miles) Choice of rough riverside path or along the roadside pavement.**
Difficulty: **Wheel chair - left along roadside footpath, up to Wire Mill Dam.**
Facilities: **Cafe and public toilets at Forge Dam.**
Buses: **None**
Parking: **Small unsurfaced car park at Wire Mill. On street parking at Forge Dam.**

From this point there are two possible routes, (though it is possible to change between them at a couple of points).

Having crossed the road, the first route on your left, through the horse gate becomes a rough path following the brook. From this point it takes on a more natural look, flowing down its natural bed with none of the retaining walls evident along its course down to Hunter's Bar. The path undulates, slowly rising above the brook and passing through woodland. After approximately 274 metres, there is a flight of stone steps on the left which runs up to join Whiteley Wood Road. Next to these can be seen the rear of a small row of cottages. These were originally to house Thomas Boulsover workers at the Wire Mill. You can either take the steps, or, at the far end of the cottages, take a path which slopes up to join the upper path by the dam wall at Wire Mill. This area rejoices in the name Bowser Bottom. Bowser is a local pronunciation of the name Boulsover, which from this point will recur several times.

The second route from Whiteley Wood Road bridge follows the road and its pavement to the left to rejoin the other path at Wire Mill. Along this stretch of road is a row of Edwardian Villas, built around 1912. This road was originally called Meadow Lane, the name being changed when the villas were built.

Whiteley Cottages

Wire Mill cottages and house

A newspaper cutting from the 22nd August 1878 has the following description of what was left of the former Wire Mill site:

"What changes time produces, for over forty years ago the late Samuel Mitchell had these works in active operation where he employed over seventy men...The last remaining [work]shop has been plastered on the outside, and transformed into a house with a garden in front, where a fountain plays among some stones.

The portion of the works receiving power from the two water-wheels is still standing. Now only the row of workers' cottages and the memorial to Thomas Boulsover remain.

Tilted rocks near Wire Mill Dam (SK311851); Rough Rock

Rocks are exposed at intervals all along the river upstream to Wire Mill Dam. All of them belong to the Rough Rock, although the rock type is quite variable, ranging from very fine, thinly bedded sandstones to coarser cross- bedded sandstones. At Wire Mill Dam, the main footpath alongside the river (not along the dam side itself), passes to the north of the cottages. At the north-east end of the cottages' property a small waterfall flows under the path. The water tumbles over a small crag of sandstone belonging to the Rough Rock. Although the sandstone is cross-bedded, nonetheless it displays a marked tilt of about 15% in a southerly direction, which is not typical of this part of the valley.

The British Geological Survey (BGS) mapped a fault near here, when the rocks were better exposed, and it is likely that the tilting is a result of slippage along the fault plane.

From Wire Mill both routes rejoin. You can either continue along the tarmac path, or climb the steps opposite the cottages to walk alongside the dam. Wire Mill takes its name from one of the trades carried on there. This dam, along with the next up-stream, Forge Dam, and the connecting waterworks, were the creation of Thomas Boulsover. A memorial to him stands alongside the dam. Thomas came to fame and fortune by the invention of Sheffield Silver Plate in the 1740s but overtaken in the 1850s by electroplating. It's said the invention came about accidentally while repairing a silver spoon. He developed a process of fusing silver and copper plates so that the resulting material could be rolled to the required thickness to be worked into a whole range of products. This meant a whole range of 'silverware' could be produced at a cheaper price than solid silver items, and this found a ready market among the aspiring middle class of the day. His original product which made him a fortune was silver plated buttons. It was with this fortune that he branched out into other things.

He bought Whiteley Wood Hall and its estate, overlooking the Porter Valley, and created dams and works at Forge Dam and Bowser Bottom. He's quoted as saying he began the work with a bulging purse, and when he'd finished the purse was all neck. All that remains of the works at Wire Mill is a row of cottages, and the dam, now a venue for fishermen. Early maps show that originally there were two dams, but at a later date they were combined into one.

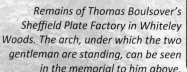

Remains of Thomas Boulsover's Sheffield Plate Factory in Whiteley Woods. The arch, under which the two gentleman are standing, can be seen in the memorial to him above.

Wire Mill Dam is the perfect place to start fishing, it's where anyone can come along and catch a roach within a few minutes, with the correct size hook and a few maggots that is. This is still the case now but the real challenge is to hook one of the large carp that have been in the dam for over 20 years. It's great to see someone catch the 16lb ghost carp and pose for the obligatory photo or two. Passers-by watch in amazement having never seen a fish so big and would never have guessed there were fish that size in a council park pond. To add to the large number of roach, perch, bream, tench and crucian carp that are in the dam, it has recently been stocked with 200 common and mirror carp. These fish are thriving and have already doubled in size, giving great sport for the more experienced angler.

All are welcome at the dam, just sit yourself down and start fishing. There's a good bunch of regular anglers who are always eager to advise you on how the catch a few fish!!

Wire Mill Dam

At the upper end of the dam the two paths again rejoin. Further along, the path runs alongside a man-made channel or goit. This is the supply for the Wire Mill Dam, and takes water from the Porter just below Forge Dam. By taking the water at this point and feeding it along the hillside, a large fall was produced at Wire Mill, accommodating two wheels of 11 metres diameter, which were said to have powered a rolling mill. Turn left where the path joins the road at Brookhouse Hill, and follow it round to the right. As you do so, look up to the left and you will see a large building.

This is now a residence, but it was originally built as a silver plated button factory by Boulsover. The buttons produced here were given their final polish higher up the valley at the Fulwood Mills. The path leads past a children's playground, public toilets and cafe to Forge Dam.

A wall built of triangular blocks just past where the path splits, and a stream passes under the goit and path.

Folded rocks near Forge Dam (SK305850); Rough Rock

The site is in the river bank on the west side of a pronounced meander, about 100 metres downstream of the road bridge over the Porter that carries the access road to Forge Dam.

The most extensive outcrop of the Rough Rock occurs on Brown Edge, but the dip of the strata means that the Rough Rock is exposed again at this point below Forge Dam. It is exposed intermittently in several river bank sections, but at this locality the sandstones have been folded into a small tight syncline, (where the two sides of the fold make a v-shape, pointing downwards). Indeed looking to the left (south) side of the exposure, the beds become vertical, as seen both in the bank itself and beneath the water. Technically, therefore, the fold would be classed as a monocline.

The monoclinal folding in the Rough Rock sandstones. The beds in the left hand limb are nearly vertical. Height of section about three metres.

At Forge Dam there is a cafe and public toilets. Opposite the cafe is an open grassed area. This was originally the site of a lower dam. The present dam provided the power for the works via a water wheel. It's said this lower dam was intended to power a paper mill, but was unsuccessful and quickly silted up.

Although this was originally an industrial works, it's better known to generations of Sheffielders as a place for recreation. In the late 19th century the works were acquired by Herbert Maxfield, a file maker. A few years later he decided to turn the place into an attraction. Boats were hired out on the dam, along with provision for swimming, and a tea-room was opened together with a playground with swings. Music and dancing were provided, but despite several attempts, Mr Maxfield was unable to acquire a licence to sell alcohol, due to local opposition. The dam was also the scene of tragedies. On one occasion a small boy playing near the outflow fell in and was drowned, and on another a swimmer got into difficulties and despite efforts to reach him, he too drowned.

Nevertheless, Forge Dam continued, and continues, to attract large numbers of

visitors. The Council acquired the site in 1939 as a gift from the Graves Trust. The boats, however, left many years ago, but are still remembered by many.

The mill pond known locally as the dam is very badly silted, but it is hoped that it can be restored in the near future. It is particularly prone to this problem because, un-usually in Sheffield, it dams the stream rather than taking water via a weir and shuttle. It is also quite high up the valley, so the stream is carrying silt from its faster, steeper, upper reaches. When it reaches Forge Dam, the full stream impounds, the flow slows, and silt is deposited. The route continues up a steep slope beyond the cafe onto the dam wall, and follows the side of the dam.

Old forge and workshops

People enjoying Forge Dam during World War 2 (1943)

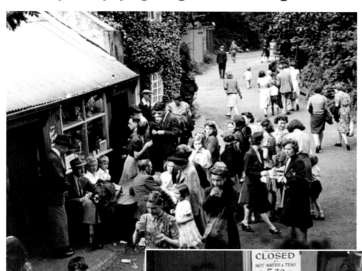

"The Holidays at Home" scheme encouraged people to enjoy themselves locally and promote local parks during the war.

Fulwood Diversion

At Forge Dam, the opportunity presents to make a small diversion, taking in some of the history of the area not visible from the valley bottom.

Walk up the slope to the dam, turn right, and at the first corner of the dam take the footpath that heads up the hill away from the dam. The path first passes through woodland, then crosses an open grassed area. In the 19th and early 20th centuries this was Brookhouse Quarry, which was later filled in and became a recreation ground. Across the road at the end of the path is Fulwood Old Chapel.

In the 17th century Parliament passed the Act of Uniformity, 1662, and the Five Mile Act of 1665, which compelled dissenters to resort to meeting in secret and in out of the way places. One such place was on the moors between Redmires and Stanage Pole, at a farm some six kilometres from Fulwood. Many of the worshippers were from the Fulwood area.

The Toleration Act of 1689 repealed most of the harsh laws against dissenters, and licences for meeting houses could be obtained from the Quarter Sessions. One such was obtained in 1714 by John Fox of Fulwood Hall, for use of his house as a place of worship.

A friend of John Fox and a fellow worshipper, William Ronksley, died in 1724, and left £400 to build "a large and spacious chapel" for the use of dissenters. This building, set in the countryside, on what became Old Chapel Lane, now Whiteley Lane, opened for worship in 1728. The names of John Fox and William Ronksley will occur again shortly.

The chapel originally stood in its own graveyard now reduced in size to a small garden. Its outward appearance has hardly changed from when it was first built, and a parsonage was added at the east end in 1754, and at some later date a schoolroom was added at the west end.

Notable in the small garden at the front of the chapel are the original village stocks. These originally stood close by at Birks Green, but were moved here when the lane was widened in 1929. They are said to be the only examples of their kind in the Sheffield district.

From the Chapel walk up the hill. Where the woodland on the left of the road gives way to houses, Whiteley Lane is joined by Quiet Lane. This was originally Carr Lane, the name being changed to reduce confusion with several other Carr Lanes in Sheffield. In the 14th century it appears in the Court Rolls of the manor of Sheffield as Jowett Hill, and the first house above the junction is Jowett House, formerly the site of Jowett Farm, one of several small farms along this lane, which here changes its name to School Green Lane.

A few metres further up the lane, past the former School Green Farm on the right, now a residence but still recognisable as a farmhouse, is the origin of the name, a cottage, once called "Charity House", which was formerly a schoolhouse.

The school closed in 1875

On the wall facing the road is an inscription

The inscription reads;

1730

Mr John Fox gave 150

Mr Turie Clerk 10

Mr W Ronksley 30

Mary Ronksley 20   pounds.

Bene
Factors
Names

Continue up the lane, and the houses on the left give way to open fields. At the crossroads, follow the lane to the left. Note the irregular, sinuous form of the field walls around this group of fields. There is strong evidence that these boundaries date from the Romano-British period, and formed part of a farmstead that must have stood close by. The largest of the group was fieldwalked a few years ago, and although nothing from so far back in time was found, there was evidence that the field had been in continuous use since at least the 13th century.

Shortly you reach a junction on the left. Take the left hand lane down the hill. This is David Lane. As you descend, you pass a former farm on the left. This is David Lane Farm, known locally as "Hole in the Wall Farm". The name is said to originate from the time when the dams at Redmires were being built, between 1836 and 1853.

At the end of the 18th century, the land in and around the valley was enclosed under the Upper Hallam Enclosures Act. Opposite the farm was a spring which was the source of water for the local population. The Act stipulated that access to the spring should be maintained, and this was done by leaving a hole in the wall.

Back to the building of the dams; the work was carried out by the usual navvies, who had prodigious thirsts. As mentioned earlier, many of the farms acquired beer licences to serve this clientele, one of them being David Lane Farm. And to differentiate it from the other farms, the navvies christened it The Hole in the Wall Farm. The farm still stands, but the hole is long gone.

Continuing down the lane, you pass a small row of cottages, called West Carr Houses. At the far end of the row, overlooking the crossroads, stands a more imposing building. This was originally Mayfield School, serving the children from the scattered farms and hamlets around the valley. In due course it later became an outdoor centre run by the Sheffield Education Department, which role it served until recently, when it was closed. It is now a private residence.

Cross the junction and take the narrow lane straight ahead. After a short distance there is another row of small cottages. These are the workhouse cottages. They originally belonged to the Ecclesall Union Workhouse, situated at Nether Edge. Inmates were sent here to raise fruit and vegetables for their fellows in the Workhouse.

Continue past the cottages and cross the stream by a small footbridge leading up to a gate. Follow this path as it skirts the field edge, passing New May House, another former farm, now a private residence. The path ends in a stile into another lane. Across the lane and slightly to the left is another stile to a footpath running behind yet another farm, Old May House Farm, one of the few working farms in the valley. This farm was one of a number in the valley bought by J.G.Graves and presented to the City. It is due to his generosity that much of the rural nature of the valley has remained. Follow this path across the fields and it brings you back to the original route on Clough Lane.

5/ Forge Dam Cafe to Porter Clough

Distance: **1.5km. (0.9 miles)**
Difficulty: **Rough path to Carr Bridge, then a choice of an unsurfaced path following the brook or the tarmac surface on Clough Lane. (N.B. The tarmac surface on Clough Lane only extends as far as its junction with Mark Lane. Thereafter it becomes rough and rutted.)**
Facilities: **None**
Buses: **83a, 120**
Parking: **On street at i) Forge Dam (Brookhouse Hill and Whiteley Lane); ii) Clough Lane junction with Woodcliffe)**

From the cafe, climb the path up to the dam, and follow the dam round to the left, leaving it and rejoining the brook over a footbridge. On the right in the brook is a

modern silt trap, intended to slow the flow and prevent silt entering the dam. Unfortunately this has failed, as the state of the dam testifies. Much of the public access in the valley is courtesy of the Graves Trust, which bought several farms and gave them to the city. However this next section of the path to Carr Bridge was given to the city to complete this part of the Round Walk by T.W. Hall, a local solicitor and historian.

Did you know

T. Walter Hall was a Sheffield solicitor who, lived at Stumperlowe, and who, after his retirement, devoted much of his time to researching the Sheffield Manorial Records, which he translated from the latin and published in three volumes. However, the records were incomplete, and he again devoted much time in trying to trace their disappearance. Quiet Lane was originally called Carr Lane, like the nearby Carr Bridge. However, there were at least five other Carr Lanes, and this was one of several renamed to avoid confusion. T. Walter Hall regretted the choice which he thought bound to be a misnomer, and suggested it be called Jowett Hill, preserving an ancient Hallam place name, but the suggestion was not accepted.

The path follows the brook through woodland to Carr Bridge, a narrow bridge carrying one of the roads which cross the valley. Care must be taken when crossing the road as traffic can be heavy at times, and the approach from both sides is via a blind bend. Look to the right over the bridge and a small hamlet can be seen. This is typical of the settlements in the valley from this point, consisting of a terrace of cottages and a separate building farther back. This is Carr Houses. It is evident from the stonework that the left-hand part of this terrace was the original building to which later additions were made. This original part dates from 1675, and was called Water Carr Hall. In 1707 this was a small public house.

Did you know

The rules concerning licensing have changed at times. The law at one time distinguished between alehouses on the one hand and inns and taverns on the other. In the past, the drinking of ale and beer was encouraged because it was healthier than drinking water, which was often polluted. So in 1830 came the Beer Act. The duty on beer was abolished, and licences to sell beer were removed from magistrates' jurisdiction, instead being made available to any householder who paid a two guinea annual fee. Such alehouses and beerhouses were allowed to brew their own beer. Magistrates however retained control of inns and taverns, which could sell wines and spirits as well as beer. Beerhouses remained free of magistrates' control until 1869.

The alehouses in the valley were mainly a response to the building of the series of dams at Redmires. The navvies had prodigious thirsts, so the farms and cottages were happy to provide the means of slaking them.
The building to the right rear of the cottages has distinctive windows. This was a penknife workshop.
The hillside behind and above the cottages is the site of what is believed to have been a farm dating from the Romano-British period. This is based in part on the meandering nature and form of the field walls. Similar wall patterns exist in the valley bottom to the left of Clough Lane.

The words on the stone read:

City of Sheffield
This stone records that the portion of the round walk from here through Porter Clough and Ringinglow to Rycroft Glen some four miles in extent was a gift to the city by the J.G.Graves Trust
1938

Just above Carr Bridge the Porter is joined by the May Brook, though the confluence is largely hidden by the trees.

The confluence of the Rivers Porter and Mayfield (SK298848)

Dark shales of the Millstone Grit Series.

The confluence is marked by a thick sequence of dark shales, which are surprisingly highly tilted and bent. Usually, folding is produced by earth movements on a big scale, but the origin of these contortions is probably due to "valley bulging". Shale is a relatively weak rock, and as erosion removes overlying rocks, the weight which had been keeping the shale under compression is removed. This results in the shales being squeezed upwards under the weight of the remaining rocks on the valley sides.

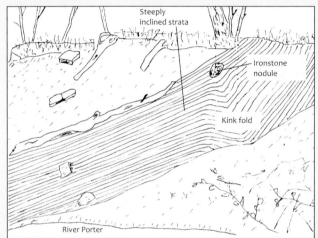

Sketch of the contorted dark shales at the confluence of the Porter and Mayfield

This site also displays very good seepages of orange ochre into the river. Ochre is formed by a complex process, starting with the weathering of iron compounds contained in the rocks. Emerging groundwater carries dissolved iron compounds in it, which are attacked by bacteria, to release the orange ochre, a form of iron hydroxide.

An ochreous seepage at the confluence of the Porter and the Mayfield

After a few yards the path splits. The way to the right crosses a footbridge and follows the right bank of the stream; that to the left joins Clough Lane, which is easier going and follows the left bank. From here the valley is completely rural, with only scattered farms and cottages, and dotted with small woods.

The river cliff beside Clough Lane (SK297847)

Marine shales of the Millstone Grit Series.

Just over the foot bridge, the River Porter flows very close to Clough Lane at this point, and has undercut the rock to form a steep river cliff on the outside of a meander bend.

The river cliff exposes about six metres of dark shales, which do not look very different from those elsewhere along the river. However, the lowest 40cm or so contain fossil goniatites and bivalves. These are invariably compressed almost beyond recognition, and all that you are likely to see are some vague spiral shapes and a few bits of fragile shell.

Both routes join after a short distance at the junction with Mark Lane. (This is the end of the tarmac surface on Clough Lane, but Mark Lane offers the ability to follow it to its junction with Mayfield Road by the corn mill, and return to Carr Bridge). Or cut across diagonally to view the Romano British Field System.

(Romano-British culture is the culture that arose in Britain under the Roman Empire following the Roman conquest in AD 43)

Did you know

The field on the left at the junction of Mark Lane and Foxhall Lane is marked on old maps as an open space called May Green. A record from 1394 says it was used for "May Games". And the area to the right down by the bridge over the May Brook is called "Butter Brigg". It is understood the name derives from it being a place where the farmers' wives would bring their butter and other produce to sell to shopkeepers who came in their pony and traps to buy from them.

Across the fields to the right is a cluster of buildings. These are the former Fulwood Corn Mills, the highest water mills in the valley, and situated on the May Brook. There were originally two dams. The lower mill was demolished around 1950 and the dam filled in, the main buildings of the upper mill are still occupied by an animal refuge.

Fulwood Corn Mills

The upper dam is still there but badly silted.

This is the place mentioned in connection with Boulsover's button factory as the place where the buttons were given their final polish.

The valley now increases in steepness. Continue up Clough Lane, which is now rough, and after a few metres there is a stile in the wall on the right. This gives access to a rough path which from this point parallels Clough Lane between the lane and the brook.

Continue up either via the footpath or the lane, and after a short distance the Porter tumbles over its only natural waterfall.

The waterfall below Porter Clough (SK293845); Redmires Flags

The waterfall can be approached from the junction of Clough Lane and Mark Lane. The waterfall is some four metres high and can be quite spectacular after heavy rain. It is formed in sandstones of the Redmires Flags, which here show no tendency to being flaggy. Instead, the sandstone shows few bedding planes and is referred to as "massive" bedded.

The waterfall and its gorge, looking downstream, from the top of the fall

Textbook pictures of waterfalls usually show a softer rock beneath the harder one that actually forms the lip of the fall, but where is the soft rock in this case? You will notice the marked difference in the valley profile as above and below the fall. Above the fall, the valley is very shallow, but below it there is a dramatic gorge, whose steep sides are quite difficult to scramble down.

In fact, the waterfall started at the lower end of this gorge some 200m downstream, near the junction of Mark Lane and Clough Lane. A fault runs through this point and terminates the outcrop of the Redmires Flags to the east.

Further up it is crossed by a small bridge giving access from the lane to the fields on the north side of the brook. It bears a small plaque in memory of Oliver Gilbert B.Sc. PhD. 7.9.36 - 15.5.05. Renowned ecologist and friend of the Porter Valley who inspired the restoration of this bridge. "Oliver's Bridge" August 2006. Friends of the Porter Valley, Sheffield City Council.

At the point where the path turns sharply to the right there formerly stood a small cottage, all traces of which have long disappeared. Similarly in the field above the lane stood Clough House, or The Clough, a family residence. All traces of the buildings of this tiny hamlet have long since disappeared, but there are a number of apple trees standing as evidence to the former inhabitants.

The geology from the waterfall to Fulwood Lane

Upstream of the waterfall, the rocks are less well exposed, but the geology still influences the landscape. At first, the bedrock consists of weak shales, giving rise to the gentle slopes of the valley sides. The thick sandstone unit known as the Rough Rock forms the prominent ridges both to the north and south of the valley. Anyone who has sledged at Jacob's Ladder, below the Norfolk Arms, will have painful memories of kicking off over a convex slope, where the lower parts of the run were quite invisible! Where steep slopes of sandstones overlie shales, there is the potential for landslides to occur, and the hummocky wooded ground of "Hell Bank" on the hillside to the south is a typical example. Hidden in the wood is the outlet of the drainage sough to the former Ringinglow Colliery, constructed in 1868. (Note, this is private land).
Another landslide can be seen to the right (north) close to the valley floor footpath, at the junction with Clough Lane.

The southern side of the valley is now an increasingly steep, uncultivated slope, which rejoices in the name of Hell Bank. Farmers in past years were fond of giving such names to parts of their land which defied cultivation.

Did you know

There used to be a Fulwood Spa, sometimes Eaton Spa, after a Dr Eaton who was so convinced of its properties that he had a basin with a canopy over it built to collect the water. Its fame spread farther afield, and Hunter records that the Sheffield Constables accounts for the year 1661 includes an entry for "Charges about keeping people from Fulwood Spaw in the tyme that the plague was at Eam". Despite its reputation, the location of this stream is now lost, and the subject of some debate. Hell Bank is a favourite for being the site of this lost spring. It has been suggested that a sough built to drain water from a coal mine at Ringinglow changed the natural drainage, and the spring lost its curative properties.

A little further, and the path and lane part company. In fact the walker now has three choices. To the right Clough Lane climbs steeply through a holloway to join Greenhouse Lane at its junction with Harrop Lane. This latter takes its name from the three fields between here and Fulwood Lane, namely Near, Middle and Far Harrop. Harrop means a place where hares abound and still gamble and box here. Before joining the junction the lane passes a copse. This was the site of Bower Hill Farm, demolished around 1968 by the City Council to make way for a golf course, which would have covered the surrounding fields.

The course was never built, and the land is now farmed by Greenhouse Lane Farm. The route finishes at the viewpoint on Fulwood Lane. This area was known as Buck Trap, which may date from the time when this was part of Rivelin Firth, a chase owned by the Lords of the Manor of Sheffield.

The second option is to climb a stile on the south side of the lane and follow the steep path straight up the hillside. Like many such paths this is called Jacob's Ladder, and the field was once the site of a ski lift operated by the Sheffield Ski Club. Nowadays it is a very popular sledge/snowboard/ and ski run. Once over the brow of the hill the path levels off and crosses between fields of the Mayfield Alpaca Farm to join Ringinglow Road a short and inviting distance from the Norfolk Arms at Ringinglow.

The third option continues to follow the brook up an increasingly steep path through a wooded ravine, Porter Clough. On the south side of the Clough, high on the hillside, is a number of terraces where there is some evidence of early quarrying, and a survey several years ago found traces of quern manufacture, probably dating to the Romano-British period.

In the beechwoods of Porter Clough itself, shales are exposed close to the path, on the north side. With luck, it is sometimes possible to find badly preserved fossils of sea creatures, such as bivalve shells and goniatites (ancestors of the ammonites). Most of the rocks of this region are of non-marine origin, i.e. from ancient river flood plains and swamps, but occasionally the sea level rose sufficiently to allow the low-lying land to be flooded by sea water. In between these episodes, the organisms had evolved sufficiently to be distinguishable from those above and below, which enables geologists to establish relative dates for the strata.

The marine band in the Clough is older than the one exposed at Shepherd Wheel. Near the top of the Clough, a stream tumbling down through the woods on the north slope has its origins at a spring in the fields above, where the permeable Rough Rock sandstone overlies the impermeable shales beneath.

As you reach Fulwood Lane, it is worth walking to the right to take in the view at the tourist pillar, and to appreciate how much the landscape is influenced by the underlying geology. As if to prove the point, a glance over your shoulder to the moorland will show the disturbed ground of the old Brown Edge Quarries, which, in their day, produced significant quantities of building stone and stone roofing tiles for the area round about.

Near the top of the Clough there is yet another parting of the ways. A footbridge crosses the brook and a path climbs steeply up the side leading to a public car park on Fulwood Lane. Otherwise the path continues to the head of the clough to join Fulwood Lane by the hairpin bend.

The area around here is not without its prehistory. Some years ago a moorland fire near the quarries revealed the traces of a temporary camp where Neolithic hunters had paused to work on their flint implements, and near Ringinglow village a flint knife and axehead have been found.

From here the headstream of the Porter is culverted under the road, but above it continues across the fields of Brown Edge Farm to its source near the sphagnum bog on the watershed above Ringinglow at Rud Hill. A public footpath from a stile opposite the top of Greenhouse Lane crosses the brook before turning south to pass by Brown Edge quarries to join the road opposite Lady Canning's Plantation.

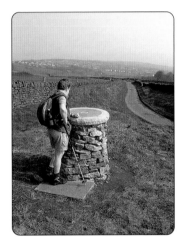

The viewing table at the junction of Greenhouse Lane and Fulwood Lane was erected in 2005 by local Rotary Clubs to celebrate 100 years of Rotary International Services. The table details some of the landmarks visible on a clear day.
They include:
Ferrybridge Power Station - 45 Kilometres (28 miles),
Drax Power Station - 56 Kilometres (35 miles),
The Humber Bridge - 83 Kilometres (52 miles),
Scunthorpe Steel Works - 68 Kilometres (42 miles),
Lincoln Cathedral - 67 Kilometres (43 miles),
London - 229 Kilometres (142 miles)
and Chicago - 6,187 Kilometres (3,836 miles).

The source of the Porter near Rud Hill.

6/ A Ringinglow Diversion

Distance: **5.3km (3.25 miles)**

Difficulty: **A pleasant easy walk around Ringinglow.**

Facilities: **Norfolk Arms Pub and Hotel**

Buses: **No 4 to Ringinglow**

Parking: **Houndkirk Road.**

Round House, Ringinglow Village

START: The junction of Sheephill Road and Houndkirk Road.

Walk down Houndkirk Road towards the Round (hexagonal) House and at the dip in the road, there is a signpost and an information display. Go over the stile and walk down the path to a junction of two paths. On the right is a ruined house (Copperras). Turn left over the stream and follow the path uphill to Smeltings Farm.

Pass the farm going over three stiles and arrive at the main road.

Cross the road and turn left for 200 metres to a signpost on the right. Go over the stile and after a couple of fields the path descends very steeply into the valley. Cross the stile into the lane and turn left.

Turn left again just over the bridge and continue through the woods. Turn right up some steps onto Fulwood Lane.

Turn right for 120 metres to a signpost on the left opposite Greenhouse Lane. On your right is the Viewing Table presented by the Rotary Club. Several places of interest are marked on the table from Drax Power station to Lincoln Cathedral.

Climb over the stile and continue alongside the wall, bearing left towards the stream. Climb over the stile in the wall and bear left up the hill towards another stile set in the wall. Turn right then bear left up the hill towards the spoil tips of Brown Edge Quarries.

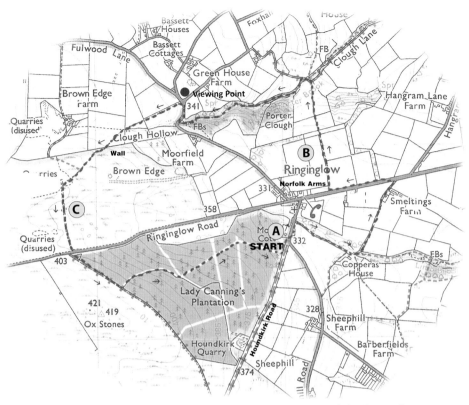

(Another path follows the wall and emerges at the source of the Porter.)

Continue along this path to the main road (Ringinglow Road).

Cross the road at the end of the Lady Canning plantation and follow the path down the side of the plantation for 250 metres to a stile on the left opposite a path on the right. (The right hand path leads to the Ox Stones then the Green Drive).

Follow the path down through the wood and at a fork in the path bear left.

This leads down to Houndkirk Road and back to the start.

View towards the City Centre

View across Mayfield Valley

Postcards from the past

A few of the many postcards produced featuring the Porter Valley.

ENTRANCE ENDCLIFFE WOODS SHEFFIELD

POST CARD

BRITISH THROUGHOUT

2544

AFFIX STAMP

For communication this space may be used

The address only to be written here

The "JAYSEE" Series.

In this wood there are open air baths for men and boys then there is a large square of sands bordered around for the children's spade to Bucket Play and water not deep beside it then further on still there is Boating on the Lake some time you will see this we hope hundreds of wounded tommies here the Base hospital is close by.

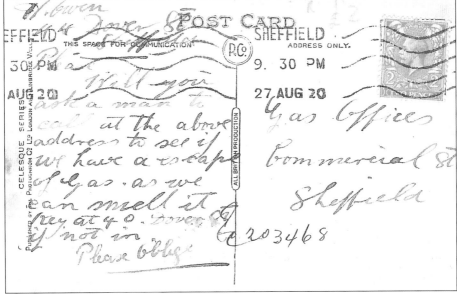

A postcard sent to the Gas Offices in Sheffield on the 27th August 1920

Please
Will you ask a man to call at the above address to see if we have an escape of Gas.
as we can smell it.
Key at 40 Dover St
if not in
Please oblige

Many happy returns dear G on your birthday, so sorry I forgot it, but I have kept so very busy & Gladys leaves me tomorrow morning. I shall miss her very much. The mothers' trip was a great success, but I was so full of aches & pains all yesterday but we enjoyed it immensely & had a perfect day & a 30 mile drive. How soon do you go to Playf*** - I hope your mother is better again. I got Mrs Wildgoose's daughter Eve last night to come for servant, hope she will do & settle down. Best wishes and many happy years & love from ***

A postcard sent to Millie Braithwaite on the 11th October 1915

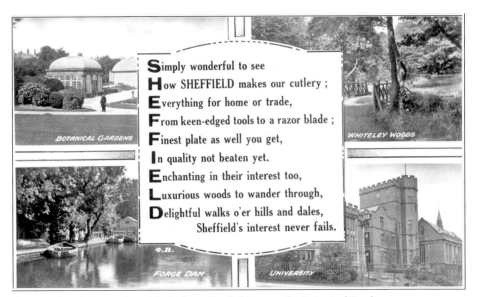

A composite picture postcard featuring a Sheffield Poem, the Botanical Gardens, Whiteley Woods, Forge Dam and The University.

A postcard sent to Percy Bales on the 22nd August 1904.

Dams of the River Porter 1855

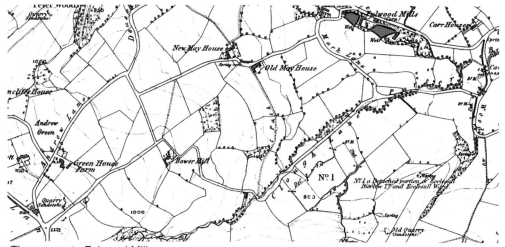

The source to Fulwood Mills

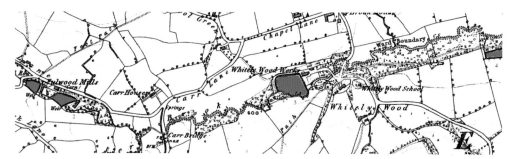

Fulwood Mills to Wire Mill Dam

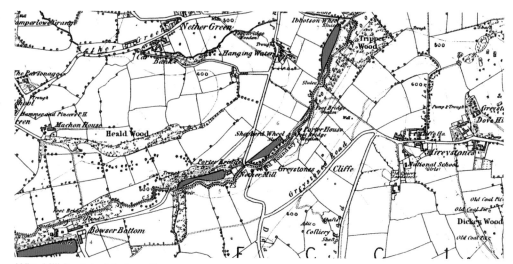

Wire Mill Dam to Ibbotson Dam

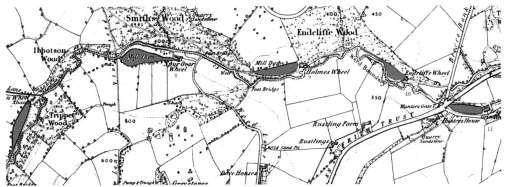

Ibbotson Wheel to Hunter's Bar

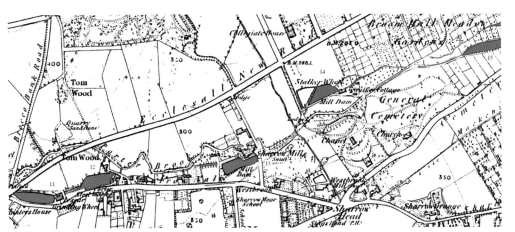

Hunter's Bar to Broomhall Corn Mills

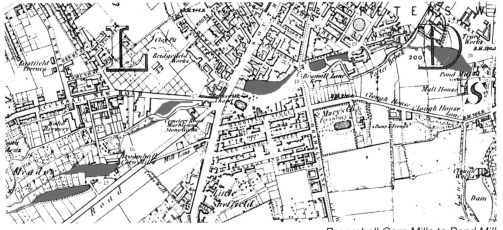

Broomhall Corn Mills to Pond Mill

Other local titles available from Arc Publishing

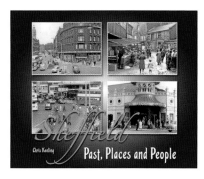

Sheffield Past, Places and People

A wonderful collection of photographs from Sheffield's past. The book has a section dedicated to the 1950s, 60s and 70s plus a great set of pictures from 1900 into the 1940s. Also included are photographs of the old Sheffield markets and some of the destruction Hitler caused during the Blitz.

Most photos have Sheffield people featured in them, so you never know; you might see someone you recognise! **£10.99**

A Photographic Journey down Ecclesall Road

This is an informative enjoyable photographic record of Ecclesall Road. Its rich diversity is well covered and brings back happy memories travelling along one of Sheffield's finest roads. This A4 landscape book not only has many photos from the early 19th century but some as late as the 1980s. It is lovely to be able to follow the route from Whirlow - seeing the changes along the way to the city centre. **£11.99**

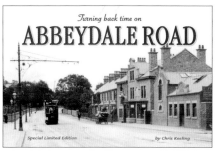

Turning back time on Abbeydale Road

This A4 book follows the road from the junction with London Road near the former Royal Hotel public house and follows its history along its four mile route. The River Sheaf flows through the dale and you will see the industries that have grown up beside it. You will also see photos of the parks, woods, halls, schools, churches, past railway stations and many other places of interest. **£11.99**

Sheffield 10

Photographic memories of Broomhill, Crookes and many other suburbs of S10.
A fascinating look back in time.
£8.99

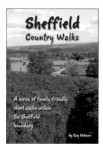

Sheffield Country Walks

24 walks around many of the city's suburbs enjoying stunning views and interesting landmarks.
£7.99

Visit our website: www.sheffieldbooks.co.uk